UNWRAPPED
MARVELOUS MUMMIES

ANIMAL MUMMIES

by Joyce Markovics

CHERRY LAKE PRESS

Published in the United States of America by Cherry Lake Publishing Group
Ann Arbor, Michigan
www.cherrylakepublishing.com

Reading Adviser: Marla Conn, MS Ed., Literacy specialist, Read-Ability, Inc.
Content Adviser: Owen Beattie, PhD
Book Designer: Ed Morgan

Photo Credits: © The Natural History Museum/Alamy Stock Photo, cover and title page; Wikimedia Commons, TOC; © Pascal Rateau/Shutterstock, 4–5; © Patrick Landmann/Science Photo Library, 5; Wikimedia Commons, 6; Wikimedia Commons, 7 left; Wikimedia Commons, 7 right; © Matthew Laird Acred/Shutterstock, 8; Wikimedia Commons, 9; © Jose Ignacio Soto/Shutterstock, 10; © Victor Jiang/Shutterstock, 11 top and bottom; Wikimedia Commons, 12–13; Wikimedia Commons, 13; Wikimedia Commons, 14; Wikimedia Commons, 15 top; Wikimedia Commons, 15 bottom; Wikimedia Commons, 16 top; © Valentyna Chukhlyebova/Shutterstock, 16 bottom; © AuntSpray/Shutterstock, 17; © ozja/Shutterstock, 18; © Stefano Garau/Shutterstock, 19 top; © Ryan M. Bolton/ Shutterstock, 19 bottom; Wikimedia Commons, 20; © Barbara Ash/Shutterstock, 21; © Louvre Museum, 24.

Library of Congress Cataloging-in-Publication Data

Names: Markovics, Joyce L., author.
Title: Animal mummies / by Joyce Markovics.
Description: First. | Ann Arbor, Michigan : Cherry Lake Publishing, [2021]
   | Series: Unwrapped: marvelous mummies | Includes bibliographical
   references and index. | Audience: Ages 8 | Audience: Grades 2-3
Identifiers: LCCN 2020030230 (print) | LCCN 2020030231 (ebook) | ISBN
   9781534180390 (hardcover) | ISBN 9781534182103 (paperback) | ISBN
   9781534183117 (ebook) | ISBN 9781534181403 (pdf)
Subjects: LCSH: Mummified animals—Juvenile literature. | Animal remains
   (Archaeology)—Juvenile literature.
Classification: LCC CC79.5.A5 M37 2021 (print) | LCC CC79.5.A5 (ebook) |
   DDC 590.75/2—dc23
LC record available at https://lccn.loc.gov/2020030230
LC ebook record available at https://lccn.loc.gov/2020030231

Printed in the United States of America
Corporate Graphics

CONTENTS

DESERT
DISCOVERY

In 1871, three brothers were **trekking** across the Libyan Desert in Egypt. Around them were rocks and waves of golden sand. Suddenly, they stumbled across a large, deep hole leading to a tunnel. They climbed through it and into the tunnel.

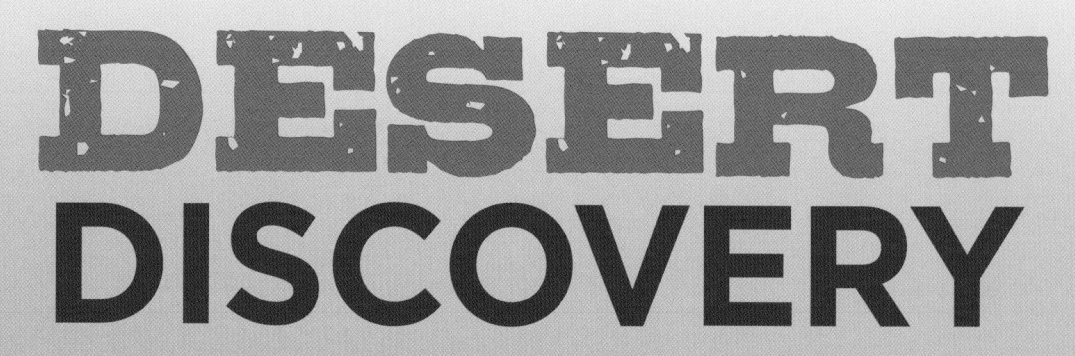

Libyan Desert

At the end of the tunnel, the brothers found an ancient Egyptian tomb! It was more than 3,000 years old. The tomb held dozens of human mummies. One mummy, named Maatkare (maht-KAH-ray), was the daughter of a pharaoh. At her feet was a tiny bundle.

The mummy of Maatkare

A mummy is a dead body that has been preserved in some way. It may still have skin or other flesh.

For decades, people thought the bundle contained Maatkare's baby. Then scientists used an x-ray to look inside the wrappings. They were shocked by what they saw. The bundle held a mummified pet monkey!

An x-ray of a mummified monkey

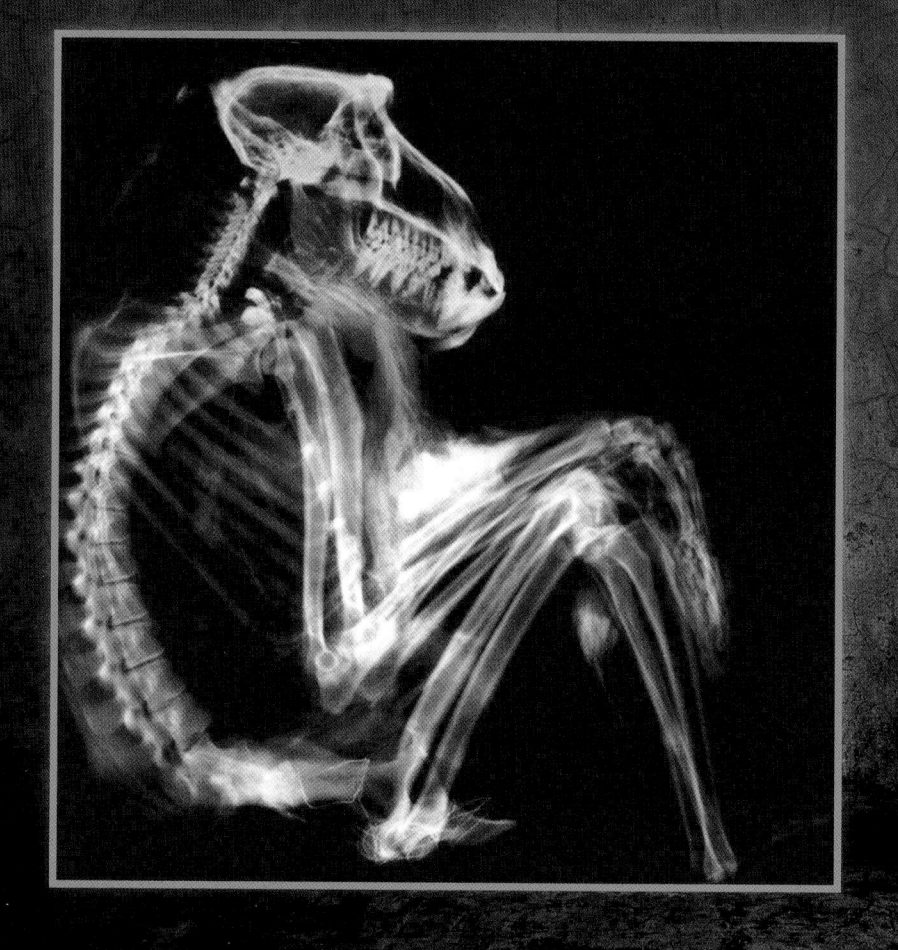

Since 1871, millions of animal mummies have been found in Egypt. Some of the creatures were beloved pets, like monkeys or dogs. Others were wild animals, such as shrews, cobras, falcons, and crocodiles. So why did ancient Egyptians mummify these creatures?

A dog mummy

An ancient Egyptian painting of an Apis bull

One of the largest animals the anci
Egyptians mummified was the Apis b

ANCIENT
ANIMAL MUMMIES

e ancient Egyptians believed that both humans and
als have a soul, or spirit. After death, the spirit lives on in
terlife. To get to the afterlife, however, the spirit needs a
. That's why the ancient Egyptians created mummies.

For ancient Eg

It was thought that certain animals could talk to the gods. Ancient Egyptians sometimes wanted to send a message, or prayer, to a god. To do this, they would mummify an animal. This was known as a votive offering.

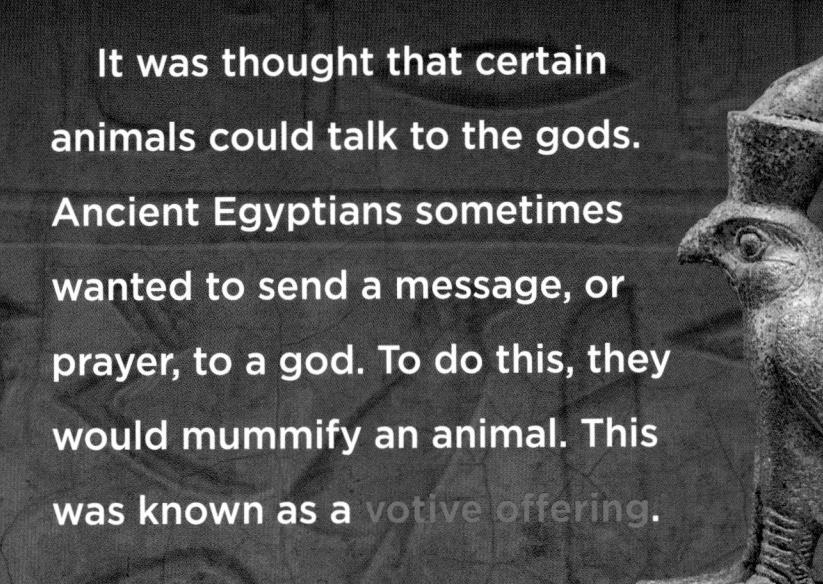

A falcon mummy case

The ancient Egyptians believed in many gods. A falcon, for example, was a sign of the sun god Ra. A falcon could fly high in the sky. People saw this and thought it could touch the sun!

9

The ancient Egyptians were master mummy makers. First, they removed most of the organs from a dead animal. The body was dried using salts. It was then coated in oils and resin, a sticky liquid that comes from trees.

A mummified ram

A pet gazelle mummy inside its case

Finally, the body was wrapped in linen bandages. Some animal mummies were given glass eyes and painted masks. Others were placed in decorated cases or clay jars. Then the body was laid to rest in a tomb.

TREMENDOUS
TOMB

In 1996, at a site called Saqqara (suh-KAHR-uh) in Egypt, archaeologists Salima Ikram and Paul Nicholson found something huge. They discovered piles and piles of dog mummies. The mummies were stacked over 3 feet (1 meter) deep!

Saqqara, Egypt

This tomb is known as the "Dog Catacombs." It's believed that there are up to 8 million dogs buried there. "The majority of these animals would have been votive offerings," Paul says.

A dog mummy

Around 16,000 dogs were buried in the catacombs each year for 500 years!

In November 2019, archaeologists made another amazing discovery in Saqqara. They uncovered two 2,600-year-old mummified lion cubs! This was the first time a complete mummy of a lion had ever been found in Egypt. Three other mummified wildcats were also found nearby.

In ancient Egypt, pharaohs sometimes kept lions as pets.

In addition, scientists uncovered mummified cats, birds, crocodiles, and cobras. Many had beautiful painted wrappings.

A crocodile mummy

Cat mummies

MAMMOTH
MUMMY

One of the oldest mummy babies in the world was found in 2007. Lyuba (lay-oo-BAH) is a 40,000-year-old baby woolly mammoth! She was discovered in a frozen patch of mud in Siberia.

Lyuba means "love" in Russian. She was only about one month old when she died.

Woolly mammoths are elephant-like animals with shaggy hair and curved tusks. Long ago, these giants roamed the Arctic, feeding on grasses and bark. Scie think woolly mammoths went extinct around 4,000 t 10,000 years ago. Lyuba is helping them learn why.

This is what scientists think woolly mammoths probably looked like.

Lyuba weighed about 110 pou kilograms). After her discovery in dogs chewed off her right ear

How did Lyuba die? Scientists think her feet got stuck in a muddy hole near a river. Before her mother could help her, she suffocated in the mud.

Artwork showing a mother and baby woolly mammoth

The frozen mud kept the baby's flesh from breaking down. Scientists also think a special kind of bacteria helped preserve Lyuba's body. The bacteria may have produced a type of acid that "pickled" her insides. Lyuba is so well preserved that scientists found milk inside her belly!

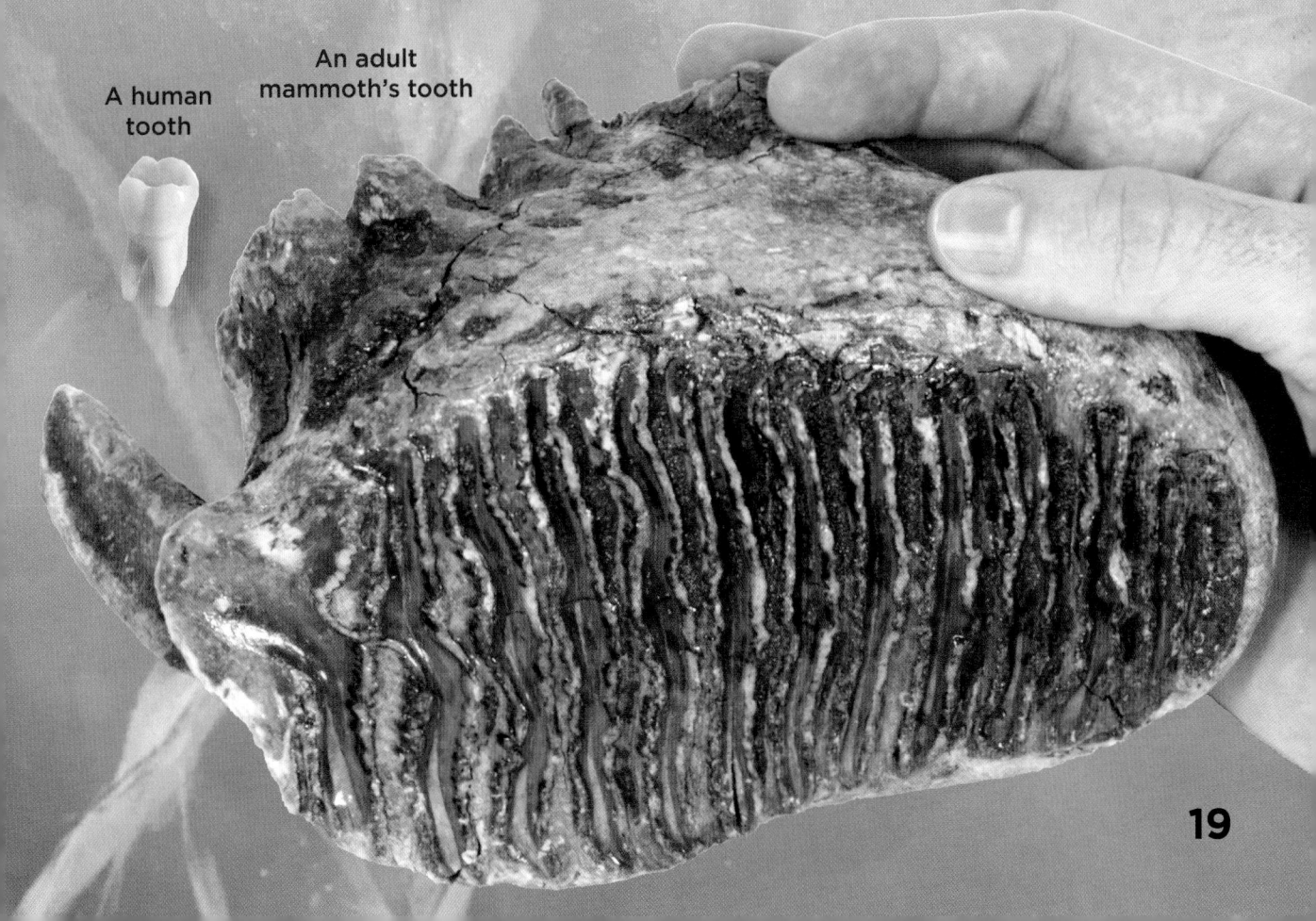

A human tooth

An adult mammoth's tooth

By studying animal mummies, scientists learn about the past. "We could see for the first time how internal organs are located inside a mammoth," said scientist Alexei Tikhonov. This allows experts to better understand how the animals lived—and died.

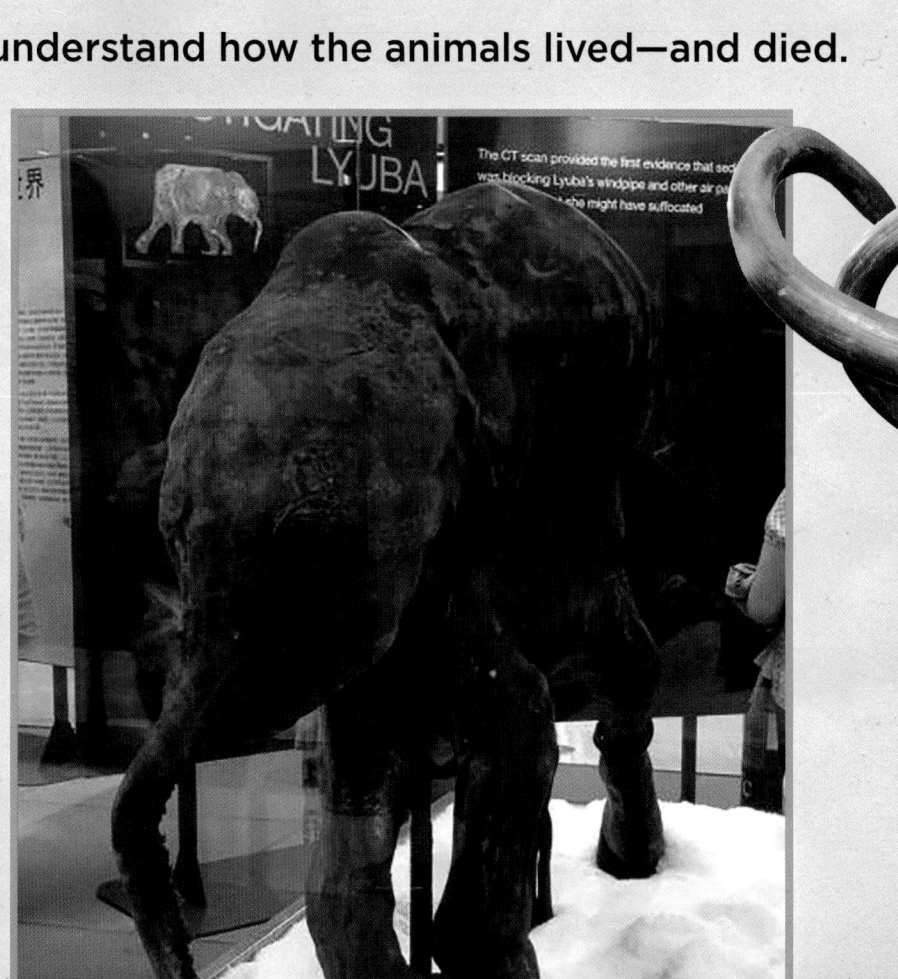

Lyuba on display in a museum

Since her discovery, Lyuba has traveled around the world! Her body has been on display at museums in several countries. For visitors, seeing the ancient animal baby is like taking a giant step back in time!

The skeleton of a woolly mammoth

Scientists are still unsure why woolly mammoths died out. The most likely causes are hunting by early humans and climate change.

MUMMY MAP

Lyuba the Baby Woolly Mammoth
38,000 BCE
Yamal Peninsula, Siberia

Dog Catacombs
About 700 BCE
Saqqara, Egypt

Maatkare's Monkey Mummy
Around 1000 BCE
Libyan Desert, Egypt

GLOSSARY

acid (AS-id) a strong chemical with a sour taste that can sometimes burn

afterlife (AF-tur-life) the life a living thing has after dying

ancient (AYN-shuhnt) very old

archaeologists (ahr-kee-AH-luh-jists) people who study the past by digging up and examining old things

Arctic (ARK-tik) the northernmost area on Earth

bacteria (bak-TEER-ee-uh) tiny life-forms that can only be seen with a microscope

catacombs (KAT-uh-kohmz) underground cemeteries made up of tunnels and rooms

climate change (KLYE-mit CHAYNJ) global warming and other changes in weather

extinct (ik-STINGKT) no longer in existence

linen (LIN-uhn) cloth that's made from a certain kind of plant

organs (OR-guhnz) body parts that do particular jobs inside the body

pharaoh (FAIR-oh) an ancient Egyptian ruler

preserved (prih-ZURVD) protected something so that it stays in its original state

suffocated (SUHF-uh-kate-id) died from lack of oxygen

tomb (TOOM) a grave, room, or building for holding a dead body

trekking (TREK-ing) making a difficult journey

votive offering (VOH-tiv AW-fur-ing) something given in honor of something else

FIND OUT MORE

Books

Carney, Elizabeth. *Mummies*. Washington, D.C.: National Geographic, 2009.

Owen, Ruth. *How to Make an Egyptian Mummy*. New York: Ruby Tuesday Books, 2015.

Wilcox, Charlotte. *Animal Mummies: Preserved through the Ages*. North Mankato, MN: Capstone Press, 2002.

Websites

Brooklyn Museum—Soulful Creatures: Animal Mummies in Ancient Egypt
https://www.brooklynmuseum.org/exhibitions/soulful_creatures_animal_mummies

National Geographic: Animals Everlasting
https://www.nationalgeographic.com/magazine/2009/11/animal-mummies

NOVA: Animal Mummies
https://www.pbs.org/wgbh/nova/ancient/animal-mummies.html

INDEX

ABOUT THE AUTHOR

Joyce Markovics digs mummies—and all kinds of curious things. She also loves learning about animals and people from the past and telling their stories.